CONTENTS

Stay safe on the internet!
When you are on the internet, never give personal details such as your real name, phone number, or address to anyone you have only had contact with online. If you are contacted by anyone who makes you feel uncomfortable or upset, don't reply to them, tell an adult, and block that person from contacting you again.

Any words appearing in the text in bold, **like this**, are explained in the glossary.

Introduction

Having a job and going to work provides money and security for a family. It also establishes a daily routine that everyone is used to. When a parent or carer loses their job and becomes unemployed, fami y life can be turned upside down. Unemployment means having no job and it can affect every person in a family.

Here, unemployed people are queuing to enter a job centre in Madrid, Spain. Unemployment is an issue affecting people and governments all over the world.

Lifestyle changes

Without a job and an **income**, it can be difficult to cope. Some changes to your **lifestyle** might be necessary. For example, you might not be able to continue with all your usual activities after school and at weekends because they cost too much. Birthday and Christmas presents might also be smaller and less expensive. Buying food and paying bills will take **priority** over treats.

If an older **sibling** loses his or her job and has to move back home, family life will change. Bedrooms might have to be shared. The unemployed person might be emotional and find it difficult to cope. Unemployment can even involve families moving to a new, cheaper home.

How this book can help

This book will explain the reasons why someone might become unemployed and who might be affected by this change. Most importantly, this book will suggest some ways to help you cope.

Unemployment affects every person in a family but there are ways to cope.

BEHIND THE HEADLINES

In 2010, the number of unemployed people in the United Kingdom was 2.46 million. Around 663,000 of these people had been unemployed for more than 12 months.

Why do people lose jobs?

There are many different ways a person can lose a job and become unemployed. A business might close down or move overseas, or it might **restructure**. This means it changes how it organizes and uses its workers, and it might not need as many people. A worker might also become ill and be unable to work. Occasionally, an adult leaves a job for personal reasons, such as wanting a career change or because of family problems. Whatever the reason, unemployment is the result. But how might this affect you?

Routine change

When your parent or carer is employed, he or she will be paid wages regularly. This gives the family money to pay household bills and maybe have some treats, too. You will be used to your parents leaving the house and returning home at certain times. They might wear different clothes to go to work, or a uniform. Your family might sometimes have a movie night or a takeaway meal as a treat, or go shopping on Saturdays. You might go to different activity clubs for sport, music, or art. All these are part of you and your family's routine, but without a job and the security of an **income**, this routine can change.

It isn't easy for a manager to tell someone that they are losing their job. Phrases like "we're letting you go" try to soften the blow.

How businesses work

When a business has a lot of work, it needs to employ more people. For example, if a factory makes toys that everyone wants, the factory will need more workers to make more toys to keep up with the demand for them. But if the toys become less popular, the factory won't need to make or supply so many. If this happens, the workers will have less work to do and some may lose their jobs. This is how businesses work. It is called **supply and demand**.

Closing down

If there is no demand for the product a business offers, the business will close down and people will become unemployed. When 800 Woolworths stores closed, 27,000 **employees** lost their jobs. It is difficult to find a new job when so many newly unemployed people are all looking for work at the same time.

Workers will lose their jobs if a shop closes down.

The cities of New Delhi and Bangalore are the call centre hubs of India.

Going abroad

If your mum or dad has a question about something such as their internet connection or their bank account, they can call the internet company or bank for information. However, they might actually be talking on the phone to someone in another country, such as India. Many UK businesses have set up **call centres** in India. It costs less to pay a worker in India than it does to pay a worker in the United Kingdom due to the lower **cost of living** there. This in turn means that the service provided by the business costs less for the customer. However, it is estimated that hundreds of thousands of British jobs have been lost in this way.

State support

If your parent loses his or her job, there will no longer be a wage coming in regularly. That doesn't mean there will be no money at all for the family to live on. When a person is made unemployed, there is usually a **payout** from the company called **redundancy pay**. This is a lump sum calculated on how long the person has worked for the company. The government can also provide **financial** support. In the United Kingdom, an unemployed person receives a weekly payment called Jobseeker's Allowance. It is not as much as an average wage, but it helps and means that families can pay household bills and buy food.

Counselling help

It can be difficult to cope with your parent or carer losing his or her job. Talking about your feelings can help. School **counsellors** are there to listen and to support you. It's also important to talk to friends about how you are feeling.

You can talk to a teacher in private about what's happening at home.

BEHIND THE HEADLINES

In the United Kingdom, more than half a million people under 35 are too ill to work due to physical disability or mental health issues. Money is available to help these people and their families cope with unemployment. The amount of **benefits** varies so the more serious the disability, the more money is given to support the person and their family.

Some people can't work because of illness or disability. Money from the government helps families to cope.

Why are the jobs in your own country affected by what happens in other countries? What are the major reasons for job losses? How can international issues affect your family?

All connected

We live in a **global economy** where banking and business are linked together. A problem in one country often affects others. In 2007, a **financial crisis** that began in the United States had far-reaching effects for workers and their families all over the world. It became known as the "credit crunch". People lost their homes because they couldn't keep up with **mortgage** payments and thousands of businesses closed down. But what exactly is the credit crunch?

When the credit crunch hit, some banks were forced to close. The banks' workers were among the many people who suddenly lost their jobs.

BEHIND THE HEADLINES

For businesses to grow, they sometimes need to borrow money (also called "credit") from banks, and pay it back later. The credit crunch of 2007–2009 happened because banks had lent too much money to people and businesses that couldn't pay it back. There was a dramatic cash, or credit, shortage. Banks stopped lending and businesses came to a standstill or even collapsed. This caused massive job losses.

This memorial in Washington, DC, USA shows people waiting for food aid. During the Great Depression, government support was given out to help people cope.

CASE STUDY

In the 1930s, a long period of **economic** decline called the Great Depression left millions of people around the world unemployed and struggling to cope. Eventually the global economy recovered and people found new jobs. Depressions do happen sometimes but they do not last forever.

An industrial process

Machines can be more **efficient** and cheaper than using human workers. They don't get tired or make mistakes, and they don't need wages. For over 200 years, engines and machines have been replacing workers in factory and **manufacturing** work. This process is called **industrialization** and it usually means that jobs are lost. Today, it is not only machines that are replacing workers, but computers too. The clothing, electronics, and car industries are just some of the areas where unemployment is rising because of new computers.

Fragile China

The Guangdong province of China used to employ thousands of workers in dozens of factories to make toys, plastic goods, and electronics. Many of the toys were **exported** to supply shops in Europe and North America. Now the demand is less because of the global **recession**. Many of the Guangdong factories have closed, leaving thousands of workers unemployed and facing a struggle to feed their families.

BEHIND THE HEADLINES

Industrialization has also affected farming. Machines now harvest crops quicker than workers can, and there are fewer jobs for farm workers. Because of this, all over China farm workers left their homes and families in the country to go to the cities for work. They hoped to find jobs in the factories and earn better wages. However, the credit crunch of 2007–2009 caused over 70,000 Chinese factories to close down. This left 20 million **migrant workers** without jobs.

These migrant workers have arrived in the city to look for factory work. Many struggle to find a job.

You can't control the weather

Farming is an occupation that depends on the right weather at the right time. Farmers all over the world have to cope with **unpredictable** weather patterns and even more extreme natural disasters, such as fires, floods, or droughts. Government money and aid are available to cope with the immediate after-effects of crop failure but in the long-term, finding a new job outside farming can be difficult.

BEHIND THE HEADLINES

California, USA, has a large farming industry and employs thousands of **seasonal** farm workers during harvest times. A recent three-year-long drought has resulted in failed crops and smaller harvests. Many workers have become unemployed because there is less work to do. The water shortage is being blamed for the loss of around 65,000 jobs.

Hurricane Katrina, job destroyer

In 2005, Hurricane Katrina destroyed much of New Orleans, USA. Properties, businesses, and roads were all so badly damaged or destroyed that workers and their families had to move elsewhere. Offshore oil and gas **refineries** were badly affected, and so were the tourism and fishing industries. This resulted in an estimated 230,000 job losses. The state government organized **job fairs** to try to get people back into employment and by the autumn of 2006, most people had found new jobs. However, in 2010, just as the region was starting to recover, jobs were once again under threat. This time it was because of the worst environmental disaster in US history, the Gulf of Mexico oil spill.

These seasonal farm workers have been employed by a farm in California, USA. Government food aid is given out in California to help people to cope when they haven't got a job.

The people behind the numbers

The main aim of a business is to make money. When business leaders decide they need to save extra money, their **priority** is not always the individual lives that are affected by these decisions. Unemployment affects people from all backgrounds, in all jobs, and in all countries. So, who are the people who have been hit by the **recession** and what happens when an entire community loses its jobs?

CASE STUDY

In 2009, Max's father, Phil, lost his job in the construction industry. Max remembers Phil coming home and telling the family his news. "He said that the whole site was closing down so there were lots of other people affected. He said the site might open up again when the **economy** improved. He told us not to worry but we'd all have to try hard to save money."

Children of the unemployed

In 2010, a fifth of British children were growing up in a family where no one was in paid work. That's 1.9 million children. The credit crunch has been a major contributor to this. Industries most at risk of unemployment are construction, hotels, transport, banking, and insurance. This is because when people are trying to save, they travel less and spend less money on housing and holidays.

Having unemployed parents can mean there's not much money to pay for activities. It is easy to become bored and think you have nothing to do.

Banking on a job

Traditionally, jobs in banking have been stable and secure. Today, people who work in banks can lose their jobs just the same as builders and factory workers. In fact, banks were among the first to suffer job losses in the credit crunch.

BEHIND THE HEADLINES

In 2008, the American bank Lehman Brothers collapsed. This resulted in 45,000 job losses worldwide. The bank failed because it had lent too much money to people who could not afford to pay the money back. Other banks collapsed too, causing further job losses. Behind every job loss is a person with bills to pay and maybe a family to support.

At least 20,000 banking jobs were lost in London during the credit crunch.

Staying ahead of the competition

When many unemployed people are all looking for a new job at the same time, the competition is very high. Hundreds of people might be chasing only a few jobs within a certain industry or town. The more contacts and networks an unemployed person has, the better.

Use your computer skills to help your parent search for a job or use a networking site.

Online!

Some professional people use **social networking websites** to help them find a job. These sites work on the basis that it's not what you know, but who you know, and they connect you to many different people. These new contacts might be looking to employ someone who has your family member's skills.

Chain reaction

In many parts of the world, towns develop in support of a single business or main factory, such as car **manufacturing**. In Japan's Toyota City, the main car factory provides the majority of jobs for the 420,000 residents. Other, smaller businesses support the factory. One-industry towns are at risk of high unemployment if the main industry fails. If this happens, it can take years for the town to develop new jobs and recover.

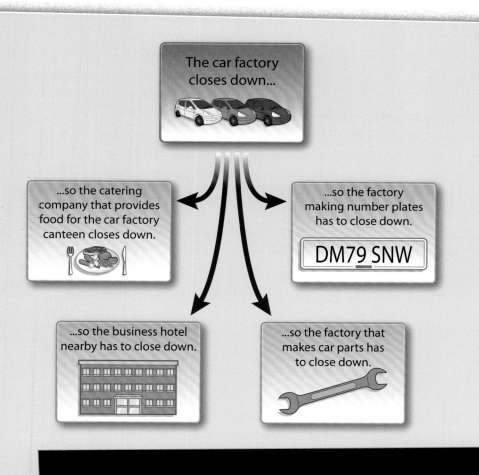

The car factory closes down...

...so the catering company that provides food for the car factory canteen closes down.

...so the factory making number plates has to close down.

DM79 SNW

...so the business hotel nearby has to close down.

...so the factory that makes car parts has to close down.

In one-industry towns such as Toyota City, all the businesses in the town depend on each other. This means if one fails, they all suffer. Most of Toyota City's workers are connected to the car plant in some way.

Sometimes a community can work together to make a difference for everyone. In Teesside, the steel company didn't want to pay out full **redundancy pay** and so the workers **protested**. They were successful and got their money, but it is still very hard to find new work because the steel factory was the main employer in town.

BEHIND THE HEADLINES

In December 2009, just three weeks before Christmas, 1,700 workers at a steel factory in Teesside in the north-east of England were informed that the factory would be closing. Local nurse Michelle Chapman said "When this plant closes there's a knock-on effect from the big people down to the little people — local engineering companies, local shops, everything."

When communities gather together to protest, it is a powerful way of making their feelings clear.

Money matters

It is very worrying when someone in your family loses their job. Lots of families experience unemployment and they develop strategies or plans to help them cope. How can unemployment affect life at home?

Sharing with siblings

If an older brother or sister becomes unemployed, he or she may move back in to the family home in order to save money while looking for another job. You may even have to share a bedroom, which might be difficult. Sharing space in the house with an extra adult will need everyone to be thoughtful and understanding. In the United Kingdom nearly one million 16–24-year-olds are currently unemployed. Today, young people are one of the groups most affected by unemployment.

Talking it over

Family meetings are a good way to discuss the challenges facing the family. The first concern for adults is usually money. Bills need to be paid and coming up with a list of money-saving ideas is often a **priority**. Planning meals and only buying what is needed, using the library instead of buying books, and mending clothes instead of throwing them away are easy ways to save money. You could also offer not to receive your pocket money for a while. By suggesting these and other ways to help out at home, such as keeping your bedroom tidy or washing up, you will be helping your family stay stress-free.

Talking as a family can help to share feelings and ideas for coping.

Changing places

Sometimes losing a job and an **income** means losing a home. To buy a house, you usually borrow money from a bank. This is a **mortgage** and it is paid back every month over many years. If the mortgage payments are missed, the house will be **repossessed** and the family will have to move. Repossession is when the bank takes the house back in return for the missed payments. In a similar way, if you live in a rented house and miss a rent payment, the owner may ask the family to leave.

Temporary home

If you have to move, you might live with relatives for a while. If this isn't possible, you might live in temporary accommodation, such as a council flat or house. Moving to a new home can be unsettling and make you feel sad. But it can also be an adventure and an opportunity to meet new people.

WHAT DO YOU THINK?

If your family has to move, you might not feel like talking about it. But have a look at the arguments for and against speaking up:

Keeping quiet	Speaking up
I can't change anything so what's the point in talking?	You'll feel better if you feel more involved with what's happening.
My parents are stressed enough already.	Your parents won't want you to worry about things on your own.
If I say anything, we'll just argue.	Helping your parents understand how you feel can avoid arguments.

In 2008 there were around 40,000 house repossessions in the United Kingdom.

New home

Sometimes, families move because a parent is starting a new job. It's not always possible to move together, so your parent might go ahead to start work and the rest of the family will join them once new accommodation has been arranged. Knowing this separation is only for a short time makes it easier to cope with. Most of the time, though, families move house together.

CASE STUDY

For some people, their parent's new job can mean a very big move indeed. Isaac Parsons didn't only move towns when his dad lost his job – he moved countries. When Isaac was 8, his dad got a new job in England so the family moved over from New Zealand. "The hardest thing was leaving family and my dog behind. I was sad at the time but once we arrived it was a new adventure. I was nervous on the first day of school, but I made new friends very quickly and I had a nice teacher. I keep in touch with family and friends in New Zealand by email."

After school clubs

If you're new to your school or your parents don't have much money because of unemployment, you do not need to miss out on fun. Many schools have free trips and most schools offer free after school activity clubs. These clubs are a good way of having fun, learning new skills, and making new friends.

After school clubs are a great way of having fun and making new friends.

Tough times and fun that's free

What happens when a parent or relative struggles to cope with the stress of being unemployed? How do they start to look for another job? What help is out there? Your family may be going through tough times but there are ways to cope.

Feeling low

When an adult loses his or her job, it is not only the **income** that is lost. He or she also loses work **colleagues**, daily structure, and an important sense of purpose. For some people, losing their job s like losing a loved one and sometimes, this can cause an unemployed person to become **depressed**. If this happens, doctors and **counsellors** can help. In some cases, the strain of the illness and the unemployment can cause parental relationships to break down. You might find it hard to concentrate on your schoolwork because you're worrying about what's happening at home. Mostly, though, with family support, the depression lifts and people are able to carry on with their lives again.

It can be difficult to keep to a normal routine and stay motivated when you are unemployed and looking for another job.

Health matters

Keeping fit and healthy will help to keep the **jobseeker** in a positive frame of mind and to give them a new routine. Walking and jogging are free activities that quickly make someone feel better. Encouraging your parent or sibling to get out and about will make them feel better about themselves and more able to look for a new job.

Lots of parks have activity trails and free fitness equipment for you to use.

A positive approach

Imagine how it feels to apply for job after job only to receive **rejection** after rejection: that's the reality for many skilled, well-qualified people today. Even upbeat adults can get down and feel as though they're never going to find another job. It can be very hard to keep filling in application forms if you don't feel positive about yourself.

Are they trying?

Sometimes, you might think that your parent or relative is not trying hard enough to get a new job. But are you seeing everything that they are doing? Remember that it can be hard for an older person to find another job if his or her skills aren't **adaptable**, if he or she is ill, or if there are a lot of people applying at the same time for only a few jobs.

Coping with unemployment is stressful for everyone anc arguments sometimes happen.

Timetabling and treats

Rather than getting frustrated with your parent, try to help them. Help your parent draw up a job search timetable just like your school timetable. Remember to put some "fun that's free" treats in the timetable too, such as visiting parks, going cycling, or having a picnic.

Showing your parent you care will help to keep them positive and motivated.

Online!

Keeping fit and healthy will keep your relative positive. A search on the internet will show what health facilities your town has and where they are. Most gyms are cheaper in the daytime when they are less busy, so keeping fit and feeling good doesn't have to be expensive.

Looking for support

Once you start looking, you'll be amazed at how much support is out there to help unemployed people find another job. Support groups can help to stop unemployed people feeling isolated and lonely. They also act as a very important network of contacts for future employment.

Jobseekers groups

Churches, libraries, and other organizations often host groups for jobseekers. These groups help people make contacts and provide support. There are online support groups too, where people can share their experiences and feelings and get advice from people in the same situation.

Jobseekers support groups meet regularly to share ideas and experiences.

Where do you find a job?

There are many places where jobs are advertised. Newspapers, magazines, online sites, and even shop windows are all places that are used. You can also find job **vacancies** at the jobcentre office.

Jobcentres

All over the country, there are jobcentres that provide support for jobseekers. A person can make an appointment to see an advisor who will show him or her how to job search online. The advisors also help with writing a **CV** and filling in application forms. They can answer questions and give advice about **unemployment benefits** too. All services in a jobcentre are free and designed to help people get back to work as soon as possible.

Jobcentres have advisors to help people match their skills to a new job.

After the initial shock, having a positive attitude to the changes unemployment brings will help the whole family to get life back on track again. It might be hard to believe, but there are some positives to being unemployed and some people actually benefit from it.

Since the start of the credit crunch, there has been a huge increase in the number of people **volunteering**. Organizations such as charities, youth clubs, sports clubs, and community projects are only able to run if they get volunteer help, and they have all benefitted from the rise in unemployment. Losing your job can result in **low self-esteem** but helping others can be rewarding and help to increase feelings of worth. Volunteering can provide skills and contacts that may help your parent or relative eventually find a job.

CASE STUDY

Becoming unemployed can be a surprisingly positive experience. One woman remembers how she felt when she found out she was losing her job: "At first I was mad and sad and scared. But after a while, I realized that the day I got **laid off** was the best day of my life because now I was free to do what I always wanted to do - start a craft store. For three years now I've been having so much more fun than I had in my old job. I needed the push of a layoff to get started."

Volunteering is often lots of fun and can create a new network for job searching. Here, volunteers are helping to paint a mural in a park.

It's good not to work all the time

Adults spend most of their time working so when they aren't, it might be the first time in years that they've had some free time. They might pursue a hobby that they've always wanted to but never had time for, or decide that now is the time to work on the business idea they've had for years.

Retraining

Unemployment might also give your parent the perfect opportunity to do something different, which can lead to a better situation in the end. There are dozens of training courses on offer all over the country, from plumbing and engineering to more creative art courses. Many courses are cheaper, or even free, for unemployed people. Concentrating on a course of study will help to keep a positive focus and maintain a routine.

This man is learning the skills he needs to become a plumber. Taking a training course may help your parent find a new career.

If your parent is unemployed, there is more time for you to have fun together.

Family time

When no one's working, family life can dramatically change in good ways, too. You might see much more of a parent who used to work long hours. Families might start doing leisure activities together, such as hiking, swimming, or cycling. Unemployment can mean that everyone takes part in family life in new and different ways.

Coping with unemployment

Coping with changes to routine and **lifestyle** can be difficult for everyone in the family, but being unemployed is not the end of the world. For most people, unemployment is temporary and won't last for long. As we've seen, there are even some unexpected benefits of being unemployed. **Volunteering**, retraining, making new networks, and taking up a new hobby – all these are positive side effects.

New job, new start

At some point, most people return to work and life settles down into a routine once more. As we've learnt, **recessions** don't last forever and new work opportunities usually come along. Most people find a new job within six months. Of course, it might take longer than that or happen more quickly.

New lifestyles

Unemployment can be upsetting and difficult, but there are ways to confront it, cope with it, and move on. Your family's lifestyle might be different for a while, or you might even have to move home. But whatever the changes, they are manageable. Keeping a routine and keeping positive will help everyone in the family cope.

No matter what your situation or experience, you are not alone. Millions of children all over the world are coping with unemployed parents, carers, and **siblings** in all kinds of different ways. If they can do it, so can you.

You will soon create your own ways of coping with unemployment and be happy.

Top ten tips for coping with unemployment

If someone in your family becomes unemployed, you might feel helpless. Here is a list of things to remember to help you and your family cope:

1. It's ok to feel sad and unhappy if your parent loses their job. Talking to a friend, teacher, or **counsellor** will help.

2. Playing with your friends and getting some exercise is a good way to take your mind off things.

3. Doing a few household tasks to help out around the house, such as tidying up or washing the dishes, will be a great contribution to family life.

4. Writing things down sometimes helps to work out how you're feeling. Keeping a diary is a good idea.

5. Use the internet, with adult help, to find free local fun activities that you can do with your family.

6. Suggest regular family meetings to discuss things and talk about your feelings.

7. Use your computer skills to help your parent or other relative to job search online.

8. Challenge your family to see who can be most creative when it comes to saving money.

9. Every evening, think of three things that made you laugh during the day and tell your family.

10. Remember that you're not alone. Millions of children and families all over the world cope with this temporary situation, and so will you.

It's important to have time to play, too. Friends can be great to talk to or just have fun with.

Glossary

adaptable flexible, easily adjusted

benefit money paid to an individual by a government

call centre office equipped to handle a large amount of telephone calls from customers

colleague fellow worker

cost of living amount it costs to house, feed, and clothe a person or family

counsellor person trained to listen and give advice to others

crisis serious situation

CV summary of someone's education and employment

depressed very unhappy

economic relating to the economy

economy system that manages money, and the production and trade of goods

efficient works well without wasting time

employee paid worker in a company or business

export ship goods overseas to be sold in other countires

financial to do with money

global economy economy of the whole world, not just of an individual country

income money earned in employment

industrialization large-scale development of businesses using machinery or computers rather than people

job fair gathering of lots of employers in one place so that unemployed people can discuss job opportunities

jobseeker someone looking for a job

laid off made unemployed

lifestyle way of life

low self-esteem low confidence about yourself

manufacturing making products in factories

migrant workers workers who travel in order to find work

mortgage money borrowed to buy a house that is paid back over time

payout payment of an amount of money

priority of greater importance

protest complain, often as part of an organized group

recession period when an economy is getting worse

redundancy pay sum of money paid by a company to a worker when they become unemployed

refinery industrial site for processing gas or oil

rejection refusal

repossessed home taken away from a buyer who has failed to keep up payments on the mortgage

restructure reorganize, change

seasonal only at certain times of year, such as harvest time or Christmas

sibling brother or sister

social networking website website that links a person with others to provide a network of contacts

supply and demand in business, how much of a product or service is available and how many people want it

unemployment benefit money given by the government to help people live whilst looking for a job

unpredictable unexpected, hard to foresee

vacancy available job

volunteer work without payment

Find out more

Books

Coping with Moving Away (Real Life Issues), Charlotte Guillain (Raintree, 2011)

Pocket Money (Earning, Saving, Spending), Margaret Hall (Heinemann Library, 2008)

Where the Money Is: Growth of Cities (Worldscapes), Sarah Irvine (Heinemann Library, 2009)

Websites and organizations

In the United Kingdom, the following organizations can offer help and support to you and your family:

ChildLine
www.childline.org.uk
Telephone: 0800 1111
ChildLine has trained counsellors who give advice, support, and information on a range of issues. Calls are free and won't appear on the phone bill. Visit their website to find out how to email their counsellors or chat to them online. You can also write to ChildLine at Freepost 1111, London, N1 0BR (no stamp needed).

Directgov
www.direct.gov.uk/en/Employment/Jobseekers/Helpapplying
forajob/index.htm
This government website has lots of useful information about looking for jobs, writing a CV, preparing for interviews, and more. It will be helpful for parents or siblings looking for a new job.

CBBC Newsround
news.bbc.co.uk/cbbcnews/hi/newsid_6110000/newsid_6110700/
6110772.stm
Visit this Newsround webpage to find out top money-saving tips to make your pocket money go further and help you save for the future.

Free activities

Free activities in your area can be found by asking at libraries, tourist information offices, or by going online and searching for 'Free activities in...' and entering your town or nearest large town. Remember to ask an adult to help you when you use the internet. Many local parks have activity routes, and some swimming pools are free for anyone under 16. If you're moving to a new town, try searching online to find out what facilities the town has to offer.

Index